D1548439

Sex Tour in a Hearse:

The Selected Queer Poetry of Owen Keehnen

Owen Keehnen (signature)

Sex Tour in a Hearse:
The Selected Queer Poetry of Owen Keehnen

Price $12.00
ISBN: 978-0-9992172-5-2
Copyright 2022

Published by OutTales
Chicago, IL.

Cover Design: Kirk Williamson
Author Photo: Israel Wright

To all the men I have loved and known
and all the men I have loved and forgotten.

And as always, for Carl.

Table of Contents

Sex Tour
in a Hearse

Things to consider:

— This tour is not a direct route.

— I does not mean me.

Communion in Heels

(St. Peter's, 1976)

Slap on parquet
Echoes in arches
Of spire & brow.
Pageantry, Grandeur
& Christ on a cracker.
Showtime in God's
Spired palace &
Heels made it real,
Gave me such life
Until I saw the looks
& adjusted my stride.

Ritual, rite, & orgy —
Bejewelled staffs.
Facial hair fetish
& BDSM martyrs,
Saints spread wide
Over tapestries
Bleeding bliss with
Eyes of ecstasy.
Saints with softcore
Swimmer builds
& bishop swish
Trimmed in red
With gold brocade.

Thought I misread
Until I met a hustler
With a cane who
Worked Vatican II &
Produced a peel apart
Polaroid memento —
Priest reclined on
Veined marble stairs
Vestment raised
To reveal his holy self,
Stockings & garter belt —
Slim feet familiar
With the angle & feel
Of stilletto fiend heels.

Real Life
(A Parking Lot, Midnight, 1977)

Two phases you & I —
Inseparable & apart.
New currents came into
Play that edged you to
A mainstream I cannot
Navigate —

Some hated us happy.
They didn't understand,
& you believed them
Over me when you knew
What we had & what
We were —

That big word was even
Yours, dropped so
Matter-of-factly I never
Suspected it filler for a
Lull until your "real life"
Began —

Wispy memory that you
Called this, meaning us,
Meaning me, a delicious
Distraction early on, but
I refused to see a future
Foretold —

Because you were there —
Warm with a great laugh
That charmed & a way
With words & lips that
Made me think we worked.
& we did —

Until real life arrived.

Whoever You Were
Wherever You Are
(Stage Door Disco, 1978)

I approach & begin
Moving with him,
Closer until he sees
We're dancing.

I've seen him around
& liked what I saw.

Looking fine tonight
Shirt undone to there,
& all that chest hair,
A tapering tongue trail
Into tight jeans,
Top button undone —
No one tells a lie
Of that size.

Lips catch the sheen
Of strobes & beams.
Closer to Whisper,
A soft kiss.
& then poppers
& the rush & the pulse
& the pounding.
Dance moves
That promise sex,
Another kiss —
Much harder
Poppers & kiss
& poppers again
Head & cock throb,
A grind to the beat

& then finding
Deeper rhythm
All our own.

By the time
The song
Beats & blends
Into the next
We're outside.

He lives above
A peep show place
Two blocks away
Up steep stairs
To a strange smell,
A broken bed
& a one-eyed cat.

We don't do names
Though he does say
He wants to move west
One day & adds
That I am the first
Person he has told.

Disco was Flash
(Comiskey Park, 1979)

Disco was flash
& dazzle —
In & out of
Poly blends
& platforms.

Sex lib hips
In motion,
So queer & free
& Black
Mainstreaming
It had to be
Demolished
With guns blazing.

Enraged because
The popular music
Of the moment
Was not theirs —
Did not like it
& should not
Have to listen,
Though radios
Do have dials.

The event itself,
An innocent
Misunderstanding.

"We didn't mean
To fuel hate
Or incite
A mob to riot
With our military
Gear or pyrotechnics
& certainly not
With the amplified
Rhetoric of rage."

Those good
Kids just got
Carried away
With all the
Wholesome hate
& rioting
At 98 cents a pop.

Explained as satire
& intended as irony.
Clearly neither.
Burning bin
An apt standby
For the real deal.

Mob Causes Forfeit,
A headline of
What happened &
Not what occurred.
The outsiders knew,
Trained by life to
See through &
Read between.

cont. ⇨

This hate was
Not electro
Hypno fuelled,
& never about
Any beat count.
It took aim at
Joy & still does
With willful
Ignorance &
A golden cross
To beat silent
Different voices
& other beats
Until there's
No more other
To despise.

That's the real
End game
& admission to
That party
Is still
Dirt cheap.

Theater of the Absurd
(Newberry Theater, 1979)

Eyes flit her to him,
Him to her,
& back again.
So much to
Misconstrue & no
Margin for error —

So I chose
A nameless world
Of upturned collars
Swallowed in the buzz
Of 24-hour bulbs.
Cash through the hole
For a ticket to deny
Everything else.

Dark theater thrills —
Shit sound, stale air,
& popcorn
Mostly for show.
(Though not bad).
A stuttering frame
Lights the off screen
Silhouettes in motion,
Seats creak & a rustle
As thrill passes
Through to shoes
That slide & stick.

Closer to the pale
& flicker as
Linen gods blur
Into luminous
Movement.

cont. ⇨

A squeaking seat,
Face in shadow —
Zipper down
Fly wide.

With the engorged
Invitation I turn
From a glow obscured
& slide into shadow.

Bessie Smith Days
(Us, life, 1979)

You live in our
Bessie Smith days
Of Ouija & speed
& chain-smoking —
Intense coffee
Conversations
That led to cups
& pots & lots
Of booze.
Binge & blur
Became bohemia.

All my organs
Carry scars
Of you:
Liver, cock,
& kidneys;
Lungs, brain,
& heart.
Milky snapshots
To capture a bit
Of death;
Each demise
A kind of ecstasy.

cont. ⇨

Scarred
Our first night —
A fall from
Platform bed
Onto a candlestick —
A death befitting
An artist,
Though I only
Partied like Poe.
It was the 70s
So you licked
The blood away
Until hurt
Turned to ache.

A door opened
On your Wizard
Den of charms —
Skulls, knives,
& snuffers —
Hides as rugs
& the heads of
A buffalo & antelope
We draped in drag —
& called
Naomi & Vi.

Surroundings
So sacred
We wore robes
& called spirits
Like naughty monks
Nursing hangovers.

Days of bourbon
& Bessie Smith,
Vinyl sparks
Turning pain to art.
You said, "Pain is
Always easier
With a translator."

We found love
In your Wilde salon
Days broken only
By server jobs.
A sanctuary
You & I —
Young & strung
To little but us
& this & drama,
Of course.
I told you lies
That were truth
& you lectured
More than
You listened.

So real & bright
& yet cooling
So suddenly.
Sad as any song
Bessie recorded.

One night you
Just stumbled
Into oblivion.
Gone —

cont. ⇨

But not quite.
At times
The needle
Still skips
To you
& through
Scratch & spark
I remember us
& there & then —
Now & again
Now & again
Now & again.

Workman Hands
(Late night stroll, 1980)

Workman hands, eager & bold.
A musky hunger & a touch so fine
My breath comes as gasps & a rush
From words to moans of mating,
Deep enough to hide the rough.
Wanting to be held in his inked arms
& to obey as surely as gravity.
Fur unfurled upon jaws, across chests,
In pits, over haunches, & below the belt.
Red meat of my heart pumping free.
Hunger of this sort leaves a mark.

The Bushes
(Lincoln Park Bushes, 1980)

We come at night
To cruise & use
One another.
Walkways of men
Headed nowhere.

Under a branch
& into the bush —
Shadow & body
Form & sensation
Blend with the
Hushed crunch of
Underbrush.

There are others.
Invisible at first
As eyes adjust,
Born of air
& night alive
With motion
& with need.

Emboldened
& hungry —
An assured hand,
A mustache nuzzle
Teasing nerves
Along my neck.

Shaggy hair
But little else
As he drops
To his knees —
Undoes my belt
& slides
Them down.

Another set
Of arms encircle
From behind.
A low voice
Growls at my ear,
In a language
Before words.

Passing lights
Run with night —
Lake Shore Drive,
Distant but alive.

Wind in the trees.
& passing feet
& the moan
& shuffle of
Those around.

The lagoon
& the park
& comrades
In the dark —
A nightly
Carnal ride.

cont. ⇨

Unseen mostly,
Invisible to those
Who never stray
From walkway
To the bushes
Or the shadows
Of stone statues.

The Statue
In the Park

(Park off of Fullerton, 1980)

Cars cruise near
The statue in the park —
An Impala in particular
As we step from the dark
To the man in the car.
Best to move slow
With cops how they are.
The door swings wide
& hotshot Cal
Slides inside &
Flips us so long as
The Impala backs
From a spot in
The overgrown lot —
Destination unknown.

235B
(Halsted Street, 1981)

Gray light plays
Beneath the
Door of 235B.
No voices there
Are real —
Just scored &
Heard secondhand
Through snow.

Lily was there
Longer than anyone —
Hold over from
A previous landlord.
No one knew
How long ago,
Not even Lily.

Black poodle-cut
Wig worn as a cap
& ladies deck shoes
From Woolworths
Whenever she left
For market & home,
Most times by 10AM.

Her cart squeaks
In the hall & a flash
Of blue housedress
As the door closes
& a chain slides
Firmly into place
So the scored
Voices can resume.
Sometimes Lily
Talks to them.

We share walls.

One day
She retrieved
A stack of
Enormous
Work shirts,
Coffee & sweat
Stained by
A long dead
Husband,
"For you,"
She said.

Lily had
A parakeet
Named Susan
That I never
Heard & only
Saw in a picture.
Lily shared
News of Susan
Like a secret,
Though pets
Were allowed.

cont. ⇨

Sometimes I
Surprised Lily
With something
From her
Beloved Sara Lee
& she told me
Strange things.

Lily said
Sometimes
When the sun
Shone just so
She saw things
Near her couch,
But refused to
Say what.

Another Sara Lee
Coffee Cake
& yellow fuzzy
Slip-ons from
Woolworths.

Lily had a price.

"Ghosts?"
I said.

Head shaken
At the word
Lily looked me
Dead in the eye
& said some
Come from
The future.

For reasons
Unknown I
Wondered if
She meant me.

She didn't explain
& I didn't ask.

That autumn
I moved &
The building
Sold in spring.
Local real estate
Was booming —
Money made
Hand over fist
With condo
Conversions.

Self-involved
Or maybe
Other-involved
With a new
Toxic guy —
No thought
About Lily
Until I saw
The building
Razed in May
To make way for
Something that
Should have
Stood in line.

cont. ⇨

Decades older
With decks
Of regrets &
Lily is there.
I wonder if
She found another
World of dancing
Gray light where
A phantom
Parakeet trilled —
A place where
Some arrived
Riding sunbeams
& others appeared
In the chop
& the flicker
Of an old Zenith.

Call Me Cliché
(Lakeview, 1989)

Call me cliché
A stereotype —
A cock hound,
A promiscuous
Silly queen.

All true —
Yet nothing
Learned or
Aped but a
Natural State.

Born blasé
With wit
~~& verbal flair,~~
Definite p.o.v.
Strong aesthetics,
& a keen
Fashion eye.

& from Bugs
To Adoring
Judy & Marilyn,
Diana & Cher
& sequins &
Spotlight magic.

cont. ⇨

Began smoking
To be Bette Davis.
While cruising
Men's underwear
Catalogues —
Buckle your harness
It's going to be
A bumpy night.

Cowboys
In tight pants,
Gladiators, bikers,
Surfers, lifeguards,
Rough trade,
& Auntie Mame.

Feyness bold
As a neon boa.
Stance & walk
Gestures & talk,
Closet door
Of tinsel,
Each entry
An entrance,
Wisdom cried to
Clamp my mouth,
& strap my hands,
& disappear.

Life sucked
But you learn
A lot as an outlaw.

Being me
Brought heat &
Though seen
As sissy weak
I grew tougher
Than most.

Some prefer
Me muffled
& dimmed
So as not
To ruin it
For everyone
Because of what
They hate
In themselves.

Fuck off!
We are not alike.
This is not
Trim but core
Of those born
To otherness —
A divine state
Of cliché &
A path few have
The calling
Or balls to tread.

Arcadia
(Off Interstate 94, 1988)

A different
Sort of Arcadia
Off the highway,
A back gravel lot
For discretion
So part-time
Husbands
In business
Grays can
Muster courage
Behind sunglasses
& beneath ball caps.

A jingle to enter.
"That's a buck,"
The zombie says
Not looking.
Then back to
Snowy monitors
Or disc mirrors
Or maybe the wall.
Glossies catch
A yellowed trail
Of bulbs
Same seedy shade
As the No Pest Strip
Near the door —
Death metal plays
At a surprisingly
Considerate level.

Marital aids
& other toys.
VHS of all sorts,
Splayed & stickered
To tease & please
In a discount bin.
Sleeved paperbacks
& a plastic-pouch
Galaxy of nasty
Hung from pegboard
& set behind
Smudged glass.

Beyond the curtain
The dark arcade —
Feral-eyed men
Lingering, posing,
& lazy smoking
Beside plywood
Booths & on either
Side of the
Cigarette machine.

STOP
Before entry!
Tokens Required!
STOP!
This means you!
ABSOLUTELY
NO EXCEPTIONS!

Car math means
A likely six
In the arcade.
Those who
Come to Arcadia
Come alone.

cont. ⇨

Tokens in hand
I pass through
Awkward
Turnstile twirl
To a world
Of partition
& promise.

A latch lifts &
All eyes slide
From me to the
Buckle of one
& then two
Emerging men.
A third pops
From the booth
Beside them
Like a beacon
Of spring.

Energy shifts &
Two others hook
Eyes so tight
I see lines
Between them
As they enter
Booths #7 & #8.
The voyeur ducks
Quick into #9.

This life so
Pure & eloquent.
I pull a smoke
As incense lit
In a sacred place
Where dick is king
& glory is used
For one reason &
One Reason only.

Sunday Robe
(Lakeview, 1982)

Slip on a Sunday robe
Silk makes you ooze
Tickles each ass hair
& licks cocoa nubs.

Back with coffee,
Erection on display
As flesh rolled
From your soul.

That hooded priest
Now in frilly collar
& about to spout
A nasty sermon.

This pillar worshiping
Snake handler who
Speaks in Tongues
Is eager to service.

Already on my knees
& ready to please,
So lie back & let me
Show you the divine.

A Haunting Uptown
(The Uptown Theater, 1996)

Uptown ghosts of glitter & foam
& in my eyes no one is home
To the thump at door or floor
Of this cavern of a show palace.
Vaulted strobes & lasers slice
Shirtless sweaty men in motion.
Some in underwear & some not,
Packed tight skin at the touch
& being touched everywhere.
Best on the alphabet soup
We swallow to glow & shine.
No velvet ropes can rein us
From this grand shrouded shell.
Unreal with dark perfection —
Staircase strewn with
Plaster pieces of a painted sky,
Fountains & gardens curl
From crumbling walls, &
Regal red carpet dulled
By age & the trudging dead.
A flash brings me back
As our mouths connect &
Crotches grind & someone asks,
"Does this thing benefit AIDS?"

Another Parade on Halsted
(Halsted Street, 1994)

Lines on the route &
Loose with celebration
Well ahead of step off.
A buzz rides express
On summer's heat
Of sweat & sparkle,
Glimmering skin &
Musk for the taking.
Music & go-go boys,
Drag & gowns &
Dykes on bikes —
Topless lesbians,
Floating queens,
& leather daddies.
Butts & bulges
Underlined & defined —
Gyration nation
Vibrant flourish
Of Pagan & pure
An endless sweaty
Flesh salon of
"Check him out"
& "He is so hot"
Amid screams & cheers
Over the baseline
Veil of ecstasy that
Lands me crushing
On the crowd
& ready to tongue
The wall of men
Surrounding me.
More float & riders
Tossing condoms

cont. ⇨

& Passes, key chains
& snack bars.
Bodies blazing
In skin-tight fluorescents
As diva driven loops
Blast from everywhere
At Once & now
I'm getting hot as fuck.
Spins & dizzy &
Then good again.
Did I take too much
Or the sun or
The cocktails.
I forgot water.
Cue the commercials —
Product placement at
Captive consumers &
Marketing masquerading
As genuine support &
All in a heated swirl
With politicos greasing
Votes from the rear
Of convertibles —
Some true champs &
Others who bare
Teeth for photos
But use them to bite.
Hotter & deeper
& my eye follows
A Mylar unicorn
That glides by
A queer kid across
North Halsted,
So visibly awed
By the passing
Pride Parade.
That I know every
Vow & promise

Being made.
& this seen-it
Cynic fades
Before his shine.

Not Here To Chat
(Kitchen, 2002)

Moving in frame
Of this luminous
Room without walls
Or creaking floorboards —
No history or foundation.
Trysts come & tricks go
But first three lines —
State preferences,
Peddle pleasures
& hawk assets.
Easy as grabbing
Fries from a Drive-Thru.
A taste of the meat
& potatoes is required
To run this new race
& elastic rolls down
Smooth & winks
Become pokes
That begat swipe
In this whorl
Of never-here
Never-there
& dicks du jour
To fuck away today
In a never-never
Land with the law
Of parallel lines,
A run into infinity
Never touching.

Masterpiece
(The Body Shop, 1990)

Sauna framed art in motion —
A scene of skin, sheen & the
Sweat of three, maybe four,
With one chosen king splayed
& primed on a wooden throne.
A subject kneels to mouth
Just enough respect to be
Eventually rewarded
With spasm & flow
As the moment freezes &
Drains & freezes & drains &
The two men kiss
With genuine tenderness
Before the three, maybe four,
Reconfigure within the frame.

The Arena
(Steamworks, 1998)

They run through the air like fish,
A quick flash of white & back
Into the weeds & shadows —
Circling fast in search of food
& feeding on what hangs in the air
As others in lairs await visitors.
Easier than the bars where I
Feel obliged to drop an octave
& not my pants or to my knees
To please & polish & relieve
The troughs & trials of everyday.
Maybe tonight I'll meet someone,
But I'm not looking, tonight every
Low-slung & handlebar hung man
In this tile palace is my someone.
One musky whiff & I lick my lips,
This arena of men is where I belong.

The Busiest Eyes
(Lakeview, 2000)

The busiest eyes
Appraising &
Sizing eyes
& head to toe
& bold lies told
To your face
To get laid eyes.

Narrow borders
Bid the captain's
Orders or maybe
You prefer being
In CONTROL.

What's your type?
What's your angle
& is there a bad one
I should know about?

cont. ⇨

So much hangs
On a haircut.
Is he hung?
Cut or uncut?
Does he keep
A tidy dungeon?
Prefer clips
To clamps?
A true top
Or maybe not?
Can I crack
An egg
On his ass —
Is he hard-boiled?
Or is my guy
An omelet dude?

WANTED:
Routine relic
Seeks perfection
For purposes of
Validation
& vanity.

Some things
Sound sane
Until you pay
By the word.

No clear
Front runner
Yet tonight,
But taste bloats
As vision blurs
& a man's
Best quality
Becomes
His NOW.

Another drink
Goes down
Smooth & a few
Possibilities
Begin to appear.

Heavier stares,
A swiveled stool
Thighs spread &
A look that says,
My-oh-my
You're getting
Lucky tonight.

Trip to the Pit
(The Chicago Eagle, 2001)

Trap door rises
At the chosen hour —
Leather, uniform,
Fetish, or
Western-wear
To descend
Steep & boot-worn
Wooden stairs
To raunchy relief
With musk & man
Scent & rustle
Of leather in
A techno haze —
The air is heavy
Like the grab
Of soft sheets
In a sweaty
Wet dream.

Daddy with a cigar.
Pits to his boy —
Smell it for me.
Smell it real good.
A cross for penance,
Pleasure,
Punishment,
Redemption
& an operatic take
On the power roles
Played everyday.
Boots licked
To a shine &
Shadowed by
His brim

Daddy nods
& the boy
In leather shorts
Starts tonguing
Overdue north,
His eyes locked
Upon the man
In worship.
A backroom beckons
& promises salve
With an impossibly
Dark corridor
Of grope &
kiss & stroke,
Suck & savor.
Allow this unmasked
Netherworld inside —
Just for tonight
Let pleasure
Blur all borders.

Ghost of Grief
(The Unicorn, 1989)

He's lost it or found it.
Beautiful man desperate
To do anyone —
Steaming & famished
For flesh & escape.
Open lips & matted hair
& a stare more need
Than real desire.
He keeps hard & ready.
Watching & aching
For another something
That will never suffice
& he's in there somewhere,
But it's hard to recall
The man that he was
Before he lost Ben
& became another
Naked ghost of smoke.

The Red Line
(The Sheridan Stop, 1990)

Lights pass in the night
Weaving between buildings,
Rising & diving to earth —
A mythical serpent.
You use something similar
To lure me from the skyline.

"Look what I have here."

Careening across a cityscape
Our ghosts reflected across
A sprawling urban constellation
As clang & momentum slow
To the worn wood
Of the Sheridan platform.

Thank you
For riding the CTA.

He had a plan B.

Down the stairs
& Past the kiosks —
Around the back
with tracks above
Deeper into a steel
Support underworld
Of shadow & beams,
Bolts & mega-nuts.
Back against a support
I feel the vibration as
Our moans rise to be
Lost in the thunder
Of overhead trains.

Scrawl
(Harbor restroom, 1994)

Show it hard. Fuck me daddy.
Need a big boner, make date.

Otto is a whore.

James loves to suck dick.

Be here Sunday at 5.

Deep throat big thick dick
In the bottom of my neck.
Deep throat guaranteed.
I never get choked.

I suck my own Weds. Noon.

Stick it through.

Why you looking here
The joke is in your hand?

Tap foot for BJ.

Servicemen serviced.

People are so loud.

Cum here -->

Abortion is a sin.

Shaved balls, Make date.

9" needs release.

Honor and respect your mother.

Thick cock 4 hungry mouth.

Hot bottom action 6/15 3:30.

Only true assholes
Won't admit they're assholes.

You are being watched.

This place smells like shit.

MK + CV

Stop defacing public property.

Shoot it here.

Phone sex anytime 312-__-____.
Call anytime.
Will make you cum better than ever.
Call anytime, he's queer.

Rollerblader in green shorts —
Meet here Sun at 2 if you see this.
I'm the guy with the turtleneck.

Be here for BJ in car, no AC.

Cops suck.

3-way with me and my wife —
Leave time.
She is a Virgo.
I'm Cancer.

cont. ⇨

Lennon lives -
All we are saying is give peace a chance.

Outland Motel Room 613 5/21,
Hot action in/out no questions.

Discover pussy.

Looking to meet someone.

Tom sucks dick in pink panties.

Drugs make you get killed in a bad way.

Stroke it.
Stroke it NOW!

Trolls go elsewhere.

Freedom is a virtue.

Ball baths given - hot tongue never tires -
Nipple action too.
Guys under 40.
No Fems
Fats (within reason) ok.

Fuck you!
10 inches of thick meat.
Fuck me!
Leave time. Give days.

What is a good time?

I turn from the wall,
& the raunchy Scrawl —
Canvas of desire
Reminding me When a quick zip fix
Was high on
My to-do list.
The scent is the same
& the flame familiar
Though no longer me,
But the memory
Brings a wide smile
Of pure nostalgia.

Tap foot for HOT ACTION!

Shower Games
(Chicago Fitness, 1996)

Beyond toned,
He's shed so much
Of himself.
Ripped & shred
Til cocks
Came alive
At his bidding.
New body & person
With regular cuts
& regular tans
Until he suspected
No one immune
To his shower game
Of pits & tits
& low hand
Belly to basket bits.
Soaping for
Distant adoration
& willing to stay
Beneath the spray
Until his iron rusts
& his tone runs
To seek a kindred
Cocksman or maybe
A perfect surprise.

The Buzz of Lonely
(North Halsted, 1999)

Bleary eye
Upon a video,
I have favorites
But I prefer
Meat on
My bone
& something
To thrill me.

I step outside
for a flick & drag
& the soothing
Taste I deserve.
These things
Will kill you.
Law to have
It on the package.
Kudos to
No-bullshit vices.

Tonight the
Spark & pyre
Tempt but
Instead comes
A shedding
That requires
Brain cells
To kindle what
Left too soon.

cont. ⇨

Peeled labels
In balls & bits
Beside an ashtray
Though some
Stays stuck
Despite my worn
& aggressive nails.

Neon neediness
Is a game
Of hoops &
Scores & rings
Around a bev nap —
The overlap
Prompts nausea.

I throw myself
Through a
Bathroom door.
Is that rumble
Of laughter
Aimed at me?

Fuck them!
Unless it's flirty.
Unless they
Want to fuck.
Then, okay.

I worry they
See me stumble
& fear no one
Sees me at all.

Dear God.
Dear God.
Dear God.

Stagger away
From the sink
Without a look
To the mirror.
Tonight is
A salty
7/11 orgy:
Tombstone,
Doritos,
& jug of
Diet Coke.

Many nights
So alike —
A week,
A season,
& then years
On a tide
Of vague dreams
& longnecks,
Believing night
After night
Happiness might
Just be outside
Circling
The block
For parking.

Pleasure Trek

(Man's Country, 1993)

Eyes watch beyond doors wide —
Spread thighs & asses high with
Double-digit gyrations of promise.
A nod, permission to enter —
Cot side is an orgy hostess buffet:
Lube, poppers, dildo, & condoms.

An unknown urge keeps me moving.
Commitment issues in a bathhouse
Like the video store or to diet or not.

Behind a loud curtain of sterile —
Cloak of lye & bleach & chlorine
Are the stone walls of a deeper well
Of trysts & smoke, seed & weed,
Mildews & man-scents unknown —
History rode this settler-worn path.
The notion is a leading lure
For a lone comrade on this trek.

Wrapped tight in white & desire —
Or nothing but cocked & frisky
As spring for almost anything.

Clocks tick beyond this maze
Of desire where days begin
& end & begin again & men
Come & go & come again
As the base pumps
& more men arrive,
Now shaking themselves
Of fresh holiday snow.

Straw Man
(Lakeview Office, 2020)

Life shifts
& slips
To the deep —
Like a Malibu
Mansion
In a mudslide.

Riches,
Loved ones,
Reputation,
& all else gone
& a straw man
Stands at
A respectful
Distance
In wait.

Space was
Sacred & air
Was god &
The party
Was on —
"Love to
Fuck, but
Hate to touch."

No regrets
About being
A cock hound
& that is
The truth in
A nut sack.

cont. ⇨

Narcissus
Loved what
He saw not
What he was —
Calm concealed
The world.
Wind & wild
Warp & shatter
That fragile glass,
Weathering skin
& scattering
Hair & hard bits
& Cock & that
Whittled waist.

The inevitable
Even lays torch to
The parchment
For awards &
A gold star resume.

Another byproduct
Of a curated world,
Constructed to
Divide & conceal
The open reveal
That we are each
Varied takes with the
Same before & after.

Lost in a Loop
(Man's Country, 2001)

Eyes dead to all
But a drop down
Screen on the wall.
3—2—1.

He leans, propped —
Still but for a
Pleasuring hand,
Cock obscured
By absent strokes.
Built & handsome
& the lone show
In towel town.

As I watch
A draft moves
Over me like
A feather to skin,
A sensation
Some say is
A ghost passing
Through you.

Losing my towel —
My ego floating
Not one look.
Not one bit.
His gaze stays
Stitched to the
Flicker & fold
Tapestry of fuck.

cont. ⇨

Looping again
To blip & flash
Washing him white,
Crackle & grain
3—2—1
& flash the same
Fading fantasy.

Maybe he wants
Someone to
Guide him.
Horniness & high
Warp my take
On the loop
& the man &
How he'd feel
In my hand.

A step forward,
His dick looks
Bored & swollen
From use more
Than aroused.

Some elsewhere
Keeps his eyes
Fixed until
My shadow makes
A ghost across
His canvas.

Hands drop
From his cock
& one lifts
Palms out
Mandate of no
So I step back
To watch a bit
Until flash & blip
& the sputtering
Clip counts down
3—2—1.

Adult Swim
(Cellphone, 2018)

He messaged,
"I want to get
Naked with you.
Now.
Come over.
I need your cock."

"What?"

"Now."

"Who?"
A guy on
Facebook.

Blindsided by
The thrill
Of desire
"Can't
Right now.
Have things."

It pinged.
"Things?"

"Things.
Obligations."
I didn't say
Husband.

"When?"

We Agreed
Next Tuesday.
I penned 7:00
& his address.
The next day
I drove
Slowly by
His flat
On my way
To work.

Tuesday afternoon
A text to confirm.
"We still on?"

Dots of response,
Buoys leading
To deeper water.
"Bad week for me."
~~Adding,~~
"Deadlines, plans,
Obligations."

"Same."

Fresh string:
"Will let
You know."

Feeling foolish,
Frustrated &
Mostly relieved,
Primed & parked
In my SUV,
Denial as
Middle-age
foreplay.

cont. ⇨

Later:
"I remember you
Back in the day.
We had
Rocking sex."

Not some fantasy
Foreplay —
He assures,
It happened.

I ask details.

"A bathhouse,"
A blizzard,
Mid 1990s,
I had a room,"
He says.

Nothing &
A lot of things
Come to mind,
A bathhouse
Is its own
Anesthesia.

" . . . & in
A backroom
Once,
The Eagle
I think."

Another
Trick of a
Needy dick.
Both are dark,
Hungry places
& maybe he
Looked different
A couple
Decades ago.

The intervening
Years were
Rough on me —
A simple fact
Of scars & slack
& a general lack
That landed me
A new spot
On the gay-scape —
The pasture
Beyond desire.

A quick thought
That my need
Might be the
Yolk of some
Cruel hoax,
But that paled
Aside wanting
His words
To be true.

Fluent flattery
& want made
Me ache to be —
For just a bit,
That hot man
I once was.

cont. ➪

He texted,
"When can
We meet?"

In some
Dark room,
With the right
Pharmaceutical aid
I'd make him
Quake again.

He joked,
"I've created
A monster."

More dates
Broken by
Words of want
That remained
Only words.

In time we knew
Our need
Was not
The other
But to revive
The specter
Of yesterday.

We excused
The timing &
The holidays —
His relatives,
A houseguest,
& my screwy
Voicemail.

A text:
"Might be headed
Out of town."

I asked, "When?"

He replied,
"Next week."

Then he dialed
& we talked.

I had never
Heard his voice,
That I recalled.
Until then
He had been
A phantom
Of text.

He bitched
About the guy
He was seeing,
"I don't know
Why I'm telling
You this."

I thought
The same thing.

He asked
About my work
But he was
Walking
Or eating
& the bad
Connection
Was irking
The fuck
Out of me.
"Have a good
Getaway."

Later:
A text
From O'Hare,
"Hey, sup?
You naked?"

& just like that.
More buoys
Appear,
Leading deeper
Out to sea.

"You there?"

I wait &
Breathe & wait
A bit longer
& finally
Wave goodbye
To whatever
This was
Before moving
Further down
The beach.

Why the Rocks?
(The Belmont Rocks, 1985)

Levels of limestone,
Shimmer of color —
Red, white, but never
Blue balls nestled
In Speedo pouches.
Asses in denim.
Cocks in jocks
& a bit of naked too.
Lust & desire
Teased & fed
To wind & wave.
Beating sun warms
Every inch displayed —
Elongate & pose,
Crotch forward
Ass primed
For some liberation.
Anoint with oil
Offering to the sun
A tasty morsel
Draped over
Bleached stones
Bleeding color
Carved with symbol.
The perfect place
For a purely
Pagan release
From rules & rites,
& watchful eyes
Of snotty saints
Snarling dogma
Like specters
From high school.

cont. ⇨

Each summer day
Spread out
For the freedom —
Sorrow & shame
To bake away
On this sheet
Of sugar cookies.
This was home,
Pure & simple
A place to hang
Through sunny
Days that seemed
Never ending
Until suddenly
They did end.
Paradise is
Not eternal.
When the plague
Arrived we
Had each other.
We were more
Than sun buddies,
We were family.
& In time
The beak rose
& the dark one
Took to flap
& screech & gave
A wing-wide lift
With a shift
In a lake gale.
Dark form fading,
Shadow shrinking
Into a cloudbank.
Left behind are
Rubble & bone
But so many
Standing together,

Staring with sticks
At what seemed
A dream &
Others already
Busy rebuilding.

Child of the Wind
(Chicago, 2019)

Chatty Cathy &
Christ Almighty
& then paper dolls
Facing death
& voodoo curses —
Towels as turbans
& command
Of the wind,

Eventually joined
By network muses
Who helped me
Take a nothing day,
Make all my
Dreams come true,
Muddle through.
& take me away
From some very
Hazardous duties.

Angels dispersed
As new urges
Guided me
To revelations
Divine & salacious,
Sacred & seedy:
Hot Male Action &
Glory holes &
Blue revues,
An 18+ underground
Playground of
Freedom where
Fresh was all
& I owned 51%
Of ColbyCo.

Seasonal beaus
Sucked dry —
Love had a small
Attention span
& a big appetite.
Mostly wasted
& wanted
& easily had.
Bored by this
Current &
Then that —
Turned & pulled
Until stalled
In the calms
Of a bay
That mirrored
The sky.

cont. ⇨

But the wind
Was still
My goddess
Gifting confidence
& inspiration
When I listen
Despite my attempts
To over chart
The course.
A rudder
Firm in my grip
Must be enough.

With hoisted sail
I feel the pull
Of a steady gale
& with face
to sun I head
in the direction
That feels most
Like being
A Breck Girl.

The Big Reveal
(Chicago, 2021)

Like something melting
Or molding really.
Body kissed by
Time & gravity —
Defiant of the social
Sneer toward slack.

Removed & retired —
Expired but the date
On the package &
State of the contents
Are separate matters,
Most of the time.

Enough preservatives
To rate a half-life
& enough survived
To scar skin & mind —
The paint upon canvas,
Divine hand upon clay.

The seized substituted
With greater substance,
Booty mostly unseen
Unheard & unredeemed.
Ushered in instead
Are phantoms of regret.

Do not expect silence.
This upright slice of decay
Is nobody's ash pot yet.

cont. ⇨

So arrogant & blind
Until my snow began
& started to slicken
A now tricky now steady
& then sudden path
Of twists until a light
In a clearing ahead —
A promise of warmth
At sudden nightfall.

Home at last
As the snow resumes
& comfort arrives as
Something so simple
As blessed peace.

Wooden Sign
(Lakeview, 1988)

The unexpected squeak
Of a shutter &
Sometimes stutter
Of a worn chain
Bring back the swing
Of a wooden sign
& a scrapbook
Paunchy with photos
& memories &
Mounting frustration
At loosened teeth
& weakened rings
Releasing stories
Dribbling stories
~~Grown boring~~
Even to me.
Can't help myself
It's that way with love.

Spawn of wood & wall,
Words & whatnot —
Toes curled twixt
Foundation bricks.
Needing to commit
To something & I
Did wholeheartedly:
A desperate union
Of work ethic
& emptiness &
Need for a place
To be & belong
For years & years
& in an instant seen —

cont. ⇨

As smitten secretary
Or devoted doormat,
A trusty sidekick
& rusty cliché
In my own story.
Ironically I never
Understood the type.

Blindsided & shaken.
Devastated by my
Sudden humiliation —
A naked sleepwalker
Awakened on the job.
Nothing is the same
As it was before.

This is no mood
Or sudden attack
Nor is it a flare
Sent from a rut
Deep with no air.
A place taken blame
For a broken dreams
Of vague adventure
Though I never
Thought to plan
So life shattered
& in time realigned
As the logical path
To ends unforeseen.

Suckled & reared
& proudly queered
While I plat-formed here,
Finding tribe & purpose
& beaus galore among
The ink & spine —
Beneath a wooden sign
I once thought hung
The moon & the stars
On worn chains
That screamed
With the friction
Of the wind.

The wooden sign
Was stored to rot
But took years to fall
Apart en route to
The dumpster —
Name carved deep
& wide & becoming
Mulch at my touch.
A name I once
All but claimed
As my own.

Fault Line
(Shelter in Place, 2020)

Confusion comes
Over what seems
Fuss or funk
But that's life
On the lip
Of a fault line.
Issues ignored
As core temps
Rise & pressure
Mounts —
A situation
On the brink
Until some
Tense moment
Brings to whistle
The hiss & glow
Of overflow
Served molten.
Shouts & tears
& crazy words
Then a wake of
Humiliation,
Unveiled as unwell
& doer of things
Never unseen.
Despite vows
On either side
My treatment
Has changed.
The Memory
Of each day
Lingers & swells
To belch tales

Told with toxic
Embellishment.
Rerunning
The day is
A nighttime
Torture that
Spawns pain
Sometimes
Until dawn
Breaks over
A moonscape
Stew of rubble &
Bubbled purge.
Haunted by steam
& destruction
As temps inside
Continue to rise
Until liquid fire
Rolls & burns
Once more.

Fireproof Gray
(Shelter in Place, 2020)

Drops fall from pipes
& rise as heat
& mist on a mirror
Wiped away until
The effort is too great
& air grows thick
With doubt & distress
& mounting duress.
Floorboards creak
& dust plumes spread
In this neglected wing
With windows streaked
& stained glass broken
In a moody messy ruin
Of shadow & whisper,
Belfry & widow walk
To return as a ghost
Using words stowed
In unmarked boxes
Of fireproof gray.

Lowdown Joe
(Roscoe & Halsted, 1997)

He is a tree of butterflies.
Like all those in my grove —
Since those leaves don't fall
But flit & alight & remind
With no new growth
& no more down below though
The dead husk still stands.

Somewhere in the middle
I carved our initials: B.J. + O.K.
A pair destined for fun &
Then the fun ended
With an ugly indifference.

I recall little about us but
What I do sometimes dips
from my periphery
& skims and floats about,
Gone quickly as it came.

He had a stunning penis.

Holy Fuck!
(U.S. of A. 2020)

Rush of rage
Masking fear
Of being felled
By believers
In denial with
A pious embrace
Of ignorance
That can convert
Hate to holy
Homicide.

Stealing my air
With a quick
Crucifix
To the knees —
Churchyard
Bullies grown fat
Suckling the teet
Of salvation.

Heaven bent
On harmonizing
Hymns bare ass
While showering
Beside fellow
Soldiers of Christ.

"Quite a weapon
You got there."

Pause for a diddle
Behind a scrim
Followed by
A fresh fervor,
Compensating
With more
Righteous hate.

A call to rage
& spit by
Melded minds
& swollen hands
That bat at reality
With a sign
Of the cross.

The Balcony
(Sheridan Drive, 1985)

Decades ago my
Fear of death
Dwarfed my fear
Of falling from
A cement balcony.

Priorities shifted,
Hovered & lifted
As birds riding
The shoreline.

Death foretold
As the girth
Of a dick
Or stink
Of tobacco
Or the stench
Of revelry.

Relief came
In a dream,
A deathbed hand
Scrawling,
The End.

Leaving something
Behind would
Make my demise
Both more &
Less tragic.

Egos always
Need reassuring,
Especially those
Dodging death.

Years blur
& the immediacy —
Not the need
To leave ghost or
Name remains.

The thing once me
Still held aloft
In draughts of air
Like the lift of birds
In lake breezes,
Or pages freed
Through the bars of
A 10th floor balcony.

This Sorrowful Mystery!
(Living Room, 1985)

Sex was messy & sweaty
& left me mostly marked
By a glad magic that soon
Came wrapped tight in latex.
Born for ecstasy & pleasure,
& somewhere in triple digits
When an epidemic felled
My no plan life-plan &
Buried me above ground
Beside others weathered
Smooth & tumbled cold
From circles of despair.
At bars death straddled
A stool & became a
Presence best ignored
In pill or liquid form
But I wanted dick
In my addiction.
Carefree cock is a hard
Thing to mourn,
But I grieved it, bad.
No space for mistakes
When the prognosis was
To get affairs in order.
Fear warped desire &
Pagan plans ran at the whirr
Of fast-forward since
I was ever-seeking
A face to take me
Back to that place
Before the virus
Thundered & raged
Through the ghetto

& left us swaying
In medieval muck,
Voices muttering
Tales of loss in
This sorrowful mystery.

Last Stop!
(Chicago, 2031)

Starting as a spot,
A kudzu consuming
& downing all like
A house of tarot cards.

"Let me read,
Your past instead."

Tight in the chest,
Umbrella open to storm
Spines spread where
Plump polyps hang.

Runaway springtime
Pure as hack & catch
& coming suffocation
Soft as a landing puff.

Beyond the Door:
Not the Film
(State of Acceptance, 2031)

White sheet
As a Caul,
Surrender to
A new breath
Ribs wide to ride
A passage through
Worm & flame
& sucking away
Name & domain.
Pilgrimage into fear
Gone along with
Rage & greed
& a need to leave
A mark here.

Freedom awaits,
Be it glorious
Plasma or endless
Space or a tunnel
To a fresh start.
Maybe it will be
A warm wave
Or a strong tide
That drags us
Below & away,
Or maybe
The next is
Nothing at all
& if that is so
Death is still
Not the end —
Even nothing
Holds secrets.

At the Carnival's End
(Chicago, 2031)

Facedown
In sawdust
One eye still
Hooked on some
Far flung future
Foretold as
Gospel
In an oily tent.

Painted tarps
To spark & sell
Though camp
Has long since
Broken &
Shadows laze
As cats where
Sleight of hand
Barkers pitched
Illusion & dream
With odds
Stacked higher
Than those in
The booth games —

"Step right up
Test Your Skill
Test Your Strength
Three tries
For a Dollar.
Ring Toss &
Shoot the Ducks,
Right your
String of loss
& win a prize
Easy as tying
Your shoes.
Don't you want
To win a prize?
No one leaves
Empty-handed."

The Midway
Can bewitch
For seasons.
Some pie-eyed
Sucker dies
Every Minute
Still trying
For a kewpie doll.

Distraction a focus
Until buzzing bulbs
Fade to dark
& a tinny canto
Sputters to silence
Leaving only
A trace of sawdust
Beneath the body.

Bagged Debris
(Alley, 2031)

Your angel
Closed her eyes
& moved on,
Nothing to see
But the remains
Of another
Messy ego.
Artifacts sacred
To mundane,
Mostly dross
To tie & toss
& heap
Heavenward
Behind temple
& taxi dispatch
Along a cracked
Pothole passage
For rats.

Even saints
Harbor stashes
& secrets but
Sometimes
Tracks get
Covered &
Much of what
Remains goes
To the sacred
Nomads who
Pick & Spread
The Trashed
Keepsakes,
& secret trinkets
Of a life.

Framed art
& dead plants;
Candles, cutlery,
Containers
& hangers
Porn, underwear
& more in a
Death spread
Bounty.

A clay god
Nestled on top,
Finds an ideal
Fit in the grip
Of the perfect
Passerby.

Someone's
Lucky day.

Sex After Death
(St Mary's Cemetery, 2032)

Stone angels
Perched & shrouded
Weepy winged
Sentinels poised
To lift & leave —
A skittish bunch
Deserving of
An eye roll,
Deservedly
Embarrassed
With Judgment Day
Being a bust.

Don't bother,
They're stone
For a reason.

What will they do?
We're dead.

Meet me behind
The mausoleum
When the moon
Is fat & high —
I'll be the one
Wearing a half
Rotted hide.

Lift your shroud
To the wind
As it weaves
Between stone
& greenery.

Let the eyes of
Night creatures
Be candlelight
& let us be
Bound by
The cloud of
Our incense.
An act the
Living cannot
Comprehend.

Ins & outs blur to
Something beyond
Delicious friction.

Nothing is static —
& that is a fact
As big as birth.

Made in the USA
Monee, IL
12 November 2022

17602516R00059